MINDFULNESS FOR CHILDREN

21 FUN EXERCISES FOR CHILDREN TO INCREASE ATTENTION SPAN AND IMPROVE SOCIAL SKILLS AND MENTAL HEALTH

❄

CAMELIA GHERIB

CONTENTS

INTRODUCTION

Mindfulness is a powerful tool. It allows individuals to have greater self-awareness; it increases the ability to understand their own emotions, feelings, and needs, and mindfulness improves concentration. Numerous studies have proven the effect of mindfulness, and everywhere you look you can find information on mindfulness for adults. Believe it or not, mindfulness is a powerful tool for children as well. It has all of the same benefits, but it comes with added benefit when these valuable habits are acquired at an early age.

Teaching your child to be mindful can have a wide range of positive benefits. It helps them speak their mind, better communicate their needs, and have greater awareness of their emotions and feelings. When children practice mindfulness, they develop excellent coping skills for stress and other difficult emotions. Mindfulness provides the opportunity to develop in a way that increases mental health and allows children to focus and concentrate on specific tasks for a longer period of time.

Many studies have proven that mindfulness with children can assist them with a number of other things. As previously mentioned, it can assist with attention span, enhance focus, and improve mental health.

Mindfulness can also help children develop social skills, and can even reduce the effect bullies have on children by teaching victims to understand bullies. They grow to realize that the bully is hurt and lashing out and that no fault lies with the victim.

Acquiring these skills early leads to a life time of improved mental and emotional health. Still, it can be hard to know exactly how to teach your child mindfulness. Many guides target adults, and the practices fail to meet the needs a child who has greater energy levels and naturally shorter attention span.

Mindfulness for Children: 21 Fun Exercises for Children to Increase Attention Span and Improve Social Skills and Mental Health emphasizes your child's needs. It gives you 21 easy and fun activities that can increase mindfulness in children and allow them to reap remarkable benefits.

QUIET TIME

J ust as adults, children benefit from quiet time. Understandably, children have a harder time sitting quietly to practice meditating for long periods of time. Still, they can benefit from meditating and when taught correctly, they can stay focused long enough to gain the benefits.

Quiet time with children helps them tune into their bodies. It teaches them to understand their own needs and gives them the benefit of quietness to prevent distractions that may steal their attention. If you are practicing mindfulness with multiple children, you will either want all of them to do quiet time activities at the same time, or designate an appropriate area for the children who are meditating.

If you are using quiet time as an opportunity to help children understand their emotions and feelings, it is important that you tell them that they are not in trouble. Having negative associations with mindfulness can decrease its effectiveness. Instead of making the quiet time feel like a time-out or some other form of punishment, make it fun by having specific learning tasks for the child. The following techniques provide a great opportunity for children to learn to practice mindfulness when they are feeling overwhelmed with unwanted behaviors.

1

Superman Pose

Practicing the superman pose is a great way to get your child to think about their body. Start by having them take notice of their current position. How are they standing? Where are their hands? Where are their feet? Get them to take a moment to consider their current pose. Once they do that, instruct them to change that pose!

To stand in the superman pose, children need to spread their feet so their stance is a bit wider than their hips. Then, they should clench their fists and stretch their arms in the air as if they're about to take flight. They should hold their body in this pose for as long as they can comfortably do so. Doing this will stretch their entire body. You can ask them to pay attention to where they most feel the stretching as this will help them focus on specific areas of their body and how it feels.

Superwoman Pose

The superwoman pose is a great variation of the superman pose, and you can practice it at the same time or at a different time; it is up to you. Again, before you get them into the superwoman pose, get your child to think about their present stance. Ask them questions to help them think about where their feet, hands, legs, and arms are placed. Once they are aware, ask them to change it up!

They can get into the superwoman pose by standing with their feet spread slightly wider than their hips. Then, they should stand with their hands firmly placed on their hips. They can stand this way for as long as possible. If they want to stretch a bit, you can instruct them to gently rock back and forth on their feet. Make sure they are moving slowly and that they are being mindful of all of the areas where they feel the stretch.

Picture Perfect

When children need to relax, sometimes it can help to get them to think about something else. You might simply ask them to sit in a chair and think about their feelings, or you could give them something to focus on. Sometimes, emphasizing feelings can confuse a child and make them feel frustrated or overwhelmed. Instead, give them a picture to look at.

As they are looking at the picture, sit with them and ask them to tell you what they see. If they are feeling stuck, ask them what colors they see, what objects are in the picture, and ask if anything stands out to them. You can also ask them to interpret what is happening in the picture, and see what they think about the event that is taking place. If the event is a still shot of two people, for example, ask them to tell you what they think the two people are talking about. Getting a child to be mindful about pictures in this way helps them identify situations and various emotions and elements in different situations. It can help them gain understanding, and they may relate that to their own lives.

Smelly Belly

Many adult activities emphasize breathing, and this is highly beneficial for children, too. Unlike adults, who can generally hone in a little easier, you will want to spend time teaching your child how to stay focused on their breathing. You can do this by making it fun. Call the activity "smelly belly" for fun, and then incorporate various other activities.

For example, have your child lie on their back or sit in a chair with their back straight. Then, ask them to put their hands on their belly. As they are breathing get them to focus on something. You could have them say "smelly belly" in their mind every time their belly rises and falls; you could have them count their breaths; or you could have them see how high they can make their belly rise. Getting them to pay attention to the breath in a fun way and makes it easier for them to stay focused. Children tend to concentrate when the activity is fun.

3

Once you have practiced these activities with your children, you will find that they rapidly develop skills for mindfulness. Children will develop the ability to focus longer on the mindfulness practices, and will likely be able to go into more detail about their thoughts and emotions. It can also help them pay attention to their body and mind, which is the emphasis of mindfulness practices.

SENSES LIKE A SUPER HERO

❄

The previous chapter included mindfulness practices that emphasized being quiet and focusing on the body. Now, we are going to put the emphasis on the senses and external experiences. When children are young, their senses are developing and they can easily become overwhelmed. As a result, they may not pay attention to all of their senses. They also may not realize the extent to which their senses can be used.

These practices are great for helping your child further explore specific senses. Each practice will focus on a different set of senses. Then, your child can learn all of the experiences related to those senses. They will begin to notice things they hadn't noticed before, which will help teach them to pay attention to their senses and see how much they can absorb from different situations. This is a great practice for young kids who are developing their senses, because it teaches them early on to pay attention to these senses and everything that they have to offer.

Five Alive

Five alive is a fun take on a popular practice that many adults use when they need to ground themselves and come back into the room. This practice is great for children when you are teaching them to use their senses. You can use this practice for fun, or you can use it as an opportunity to calm an anxious or overwhelmed child and bring them back into the room.

To complete the five alive practice, start by having the child identify one thing that they can *taste*. You can give them a drink or a small bite of food that will give them something to pay attention to. Ask them to talk about the taste and texture of the item.

Then, move on to *smell*. Have the child consider what two smells they can identify in the room. How would they describe the smells? Do the smells make them feel a certain way? Do they complement each other, or do they *not* go together? If necessary, ask questions to get the child to pay more attention to the sense of smell and their experience at the moment.

The next sense to think about is *sound*. Ask the child to list three things they can hear in the moment, and again ask them to think about these sounds. What are the sounds? Where are they coming from? Do they enjoy the sound, or does it make them feel uncomfortable or does the sound cause a different emotion?

Now you will want to ask about *touch*. What are four things that the child can feel right now? If you want, you can have different fabrics and objects in a box that the child can pick up and hold. Ask them to explore the textures and think about how they differ from one another. Then, you can ask if they have felt these textures before and what they are reminded of. Help them concentrate on the objects they are feeling.

Last, involve the sense of *sight*. What are five things that the child can see? What do the objects look like? What colors are they? Do they remind the child of anything? Involve the sense of sight as much as you can, and engage the child by challenging him or her to identify less obvious things instead of ones that are easily visible.

It is important to get the child to identify the five senses and pay attention to the feelings each one invokes. It is a fun activity that can be done quickly, and it helps children when they are overwhelmed or stressed; this visualizing can help them relax and feel calm. You can also use this exercise as a daily mindfulness practice to teach your child to ask the right questions to fully engage their senses.

Tastes Like Chicken

This mindfulness practice is a fun one that combines two senses. It excludes the sense of sight and includes the sense of taste. You accomplish this activity by blindfolding the child and then feeding the child a bite of different types of food. As you do, ask them to identify what they notice about the food, and have them tell you if they know what the food is.

When you are doing this activity, make sure that the child is comfortable with being blindfolded. For some children, this is overwhelming or uncomfortable, and it detracts from the experience. For children who don't like to be blindfolded, you can complete this activity without the blindfold. Instead of asking them to guess what the food is, simply ask them to tell you what the textures and tastes are like.

This activity can be conducted in many ways. You should do your best to use as many textures and flavors as possible. Try yogurt, chicken, and peas for example. Each one has a drastically different texture and taste, which will encourage the child to stay focused and consider the differences. Make sure you are aware of potential food allergies before playing this game to prevent illness or injury.

Swag Bag

An enjoyable activity you can try with kids involves a *swag bag*, or a *texture bag*. You can make texture bags using traditional zip lock bags, though you may want to seal a bag within another sealed bag to keep things tidy. In the bag, you can combine a number of things that engage different textures. Then, the child can feel around the bag and experience the differences! You can also include the sense of sight by adding various colorful objects.

To create a swag bag, start with a zip lock bag. Then, you can add water if you want other objects to float around inside. Or, you can add shaving cream or tempura paint. If you are adding the paint, try to prevent it from mixing together before the child starts to play with them. Then, for added visual effect, add glitter.

Then, you can start adding other small objects. Consider things like bouncy balls, small animal figures, and other small trinkets you would find in the toy section of a dollar store. You want to provide a way for the child to use the sense of touch. This activity is fun for them when they feel stressed or overwhelmed. Kids love to feel around for the different objects and try to identify them.

If you do not wish to add objects, you can instead fill the bag with various paints and then seal it. Clip it to a board or tape it to the desk, and then the child can run their fingers across it and finger paint without the mess!

This type of bag encourages children to think about textures and sights. It allows them to experience the feel of different things, even if you have only added colorful paints and shaving cream. They also get to see what the paints look like as they mix together and how they affect the objects. It activity includes two senses in a fun activity that engages the mind.

Mindful Melody

The sense of sound can be very relaxing for many children. Using this sense can help children stop paying attention to a noisy environment and instead pay attention to another specific sound. You can complete this activity in many ways, but the ultimate goal is to have them listen to some form of music. Then, they can start telling you what they notice about the music.

When you are doing this activity, you may choose to listen to a single song all the way through. You might want to change the genre between sessions, but that is up to you. You may prefer to play about 30-60 seconds of songs from different genres. Then, your child can pay attention to the differences and tell you what they notice. Sometimes switching it up a few times helps keep children engaged and focused and prevents them from getting distracted by their surroundings.

Swift Scents

The sense of smell provides another great opportunity to engage senses in the mindfulness practice. The sense of smell is often ignored, but it can have a significant effect on an individual's ability to calm down. You can present the scents in many different ways: candles, scented pompoms or stuffed animals, or even seasonal flowers. The objective is to get children to smell a variety of aromas. Ask them what they notice about the smells and how these smells make them feel. Are they relaxing, or do they energize? Does it remind them of something, or is this smell new to them? Ask them to consider the different smells and compare them to one another. Is one floral and one nutty? What differences do they notice?

The sense of smell has a more powerful effect on people than many realize. It is a great tool when you are engaging senses in a way that is fun and exciting. Something to consider, however, is that some individuals have strong allergies that can take effect simply by smelling something, so you will want to inquire beforehand about allergies. The most common offenders are nuts and eucalyptus.

Engaging the senses is a great way to teach children to further explore their senses. At young ages, they already have a natural desire to explore such things. By emphasizing that natural desire and turning it into a fun game, you can increase their ability to pay attention and engage in the practice. Then, you can use that practice to teach them about mindfulness. It is a great opportunity to encourage development on various levels and can help children recognize the differences between their senses. The exercises also teach them that their senses influence them in major ways and that they can bring about emotional experiences that could be both positive and negative. When they recognize this, they can develop a heightened sense of self-awareness, which is an important goal when you are developing a mindfulness practice.

SLOW YOUR JELLY ROLL

❋

Some children tend to be go-go-go all of the time, and it can be difficult to slow them down. However, slowing them down can also help them experience the different things in their environment that are affecting them. When children slow down, they begin to notice things that they weren't aware of before. This can be turned into an extremely fun exercise that helps children become more aware of their surroundings and begin to notice things that have previously seemed non-existent or unimportant.

Tiny and Mighty

Tiny and mighty is a fun activity you can complete which gets children thinking about the smaller things in their environment. "Out of sight, out of mind" is a major tendency in children, and teaching them to narrow in on these smaller things and pay attention can help them further explore their environment. When children are given the opportunity to pay attention to these smaller things, they begin to realize that their environment is much more dynamic than they may have previously known. It also gives them the opportunity to experience everything in their environment and to recognize its importance.

A great way to practice *tiny and mighty* is to go for a nature walk. On that walk, challenge the children to pay attention to small things. While they should notice larger things, too, you want them to focus on things they may not have seen before. Have them look for different types of leaves and flowers, for small bugs and animals, and for other "insignificant" factors in the environment. As they identify these things, ask them to consider the following: What do they look like? If applicable, what do they feel like? How does an object contribute to the environment as a whole? For example, leaves that fall on the ground disintegrate and turn into fertilizer for plants that continue to grow; fallen trees produce small seedlings that will eventually grow into large trees to shade and protect the environment; ants are a part of the disintegrating process, etc. Help them realize that even the smallest parts of the environment are critical for the environment to work in a successful way.

You can bring this practice into the classroom or the home. Have the child notice things that they were previously not aware of. Light switches are important to bring light, and outlets are important to provide power. In the classroom, pens and pencils help students write things down as they are learning. Encourage them to think about the smaller parts of their environment that they may not have previously noticed. Help them recognize the importance of everything in their environment and how each object contributes to the greater picture. It can also get them thinking about how *they* contribute to the environment and what their important role is.

Bouncing Balloons

A wonderful game for getting children mindful and focused is playing bouncing balloons. Fill a balloon or two with air and set the rules of the game: the balloon cannot touch the ground, and everyone is to move slowly and calmly. In other games of bouncing balloons, children may become overly excited and start diving for the balloons and their energy levels will continue to increase as they play. The objective here is to have them recognize their own actions and take control over them. By playing slowly and calmly, even though they may feel extremely energized, they are learning to take control of their actions. They learn what it feels like to identify emotions related to excitement and to observe the emotions without indulging in them. This teaches them that even in situations that may stimulate them and cause them to feel extremely energetic, they do not necessarily have to react. These skills are important because they teach them how to effectively settle down and focus when needed. For example, in a classroom where the teacher wants to start teaching but the children are full of energy, those who have this skill will know how to recognize the energy but remain calm anyway.

Heart Smart

Similar to smelly belly, heart smart is another inward practice that encourages kids to slow down and pay attention to themselves. It gives them the opportunity to pay attention to their heart beat and feel more relaxed as a result. It is another way for children to become self-aware about another part of their body: the heart.

To practice heart smart, have children lie on the floor and place their hands on their chest. Ask them to be quiet so they can find their pulse and feel it. They may even begin to feel like they can hear it if they tune in enough. Then, ask them to pay attention to their heartbeat. Encourage them to stay focused by counting each heartbeat. The activity brings their awareness to their heart and reduces the likelihood of their becoming distracted. If they stop counting and become distracted, ask them to start over again. See how many heartbeats they can count, and for fun, you can keep record of it and see if they can beat their record next time.

Star Jar

This is a wonderful opportunity to engage the sense of sight and teach a powerful lesson about mindfulness at the same time. You can start by having the child or children sit in front of you. In your hand, you should have a clear mason jar filled with water. As they watch, add a spoonful of glitter glue to the water. If you do not have glitter glue, you can add regular glue and some dry glitter. Then, you can replace the lid.

As they are watching, shake the jar so everything mixes together. Explain that the shaken jar can be hard to see through. Likewise, when they are stressed, their thoughts seem jumbled and hard to understand. With all of the glue and glitter floating around, the water becomes messy and you can't see clearly. The same is true for people with their emotions, no matter how old they are. Even grownups experience this. When their emotions are too shaken, there is no chance that they can see a situation clearly.

Once you have explained this, put the jar down and let it sit still for a bit. As everything in the jar begins to settle, move on to the next part of the explanation. Explain that as the jar sits in stillness for some time, everything settles down. Then, it becomes easier to see clearly into the jar. The glitter and glue separate from the water, and you can see through the water. The same is true of emotions. When you sit still for a while, your emotions settle and you can clearly identify what they are and why you have them. Then, you can approach the situation in a more mindful way that serves everyone instead of becoming overwhelmed and acting out of frustration or other cloudy emotions.

Teaching children the practice of slowing down is important. In these practices, they don't necessarily need to stop altogether. They just need to slow down and adjust their focus. Instead of only focusing on big things that are a part of their environment and present world, teach them to focus on the smaller things. Smaller things such as thoughts and emotions, bugs and leaves, and their heartbeat are things that they may not recognize on a regular basis. Encouraging them to narrow in on these things teaches them that even though they aren't always aware of their presence, these things are always around and they have a very important role in life. Mindfulness helps them develop a greater sense of awareness of the world around them, themselves, and the role they play in the world.

A VACATION TO YOUR HAPPY PLACE

❄

Everyone is aware of their happy place and can benefit from it even children. Creating fun practices around their happy place is a great way to take children out of stressful or mundane situations and encourage them to use their mind and imagination to activate feelings and emotions that may not be triggered by their environment. When children learn about their happy place and how to use it to their advantage, they gain the ability to experience positive emotions even if they are not in an environment that triggers positive emotions. Having a happy place gives them a wonderful opportunity to focus on their emotions and take control of them.

The happy place can be used when children are bored, stressed, angry, frustrated, sad, or otherwise feeling unhappy. It is a great opportunity to teach children to identify the emotions that don't feel good and turn them into happier emotions. It is possible to prevent their negative emotions from spiraling out of control due to a lack of understanding about what they mean and why they exist.

A Mental Staycation

For older children who are able to understand stillness practices, having a mental staycation provides an excellent opportunity to get them to go to their happy place. With a staycation, it is possible to escape to a happier place without leaving the present environment. You can use a generic visualization, either guided by you or by taped recording to encourage them to mentally visit their happy place.

If you want to guide them through the visualization, you can use generic questions that will work for anyone's happy place. Questions like, "Imagine you are going to your happy place; what does it look like? Other than happy, how do you feel when you go there? What sounds do you hear in your happy place? Are there any smells or tastes?" These questions are great to help them use their own imagination to enrich their happy place. It gives you the opportunity to guide their visualization and keep them focused, while encouraging them to think about the many elements of their happy place. The more real they can make this place in their minds, the more effective it will be at bringing peace and happiness to them.

Some children may find it difficult to meditate or visualize for too long, so don't make them feel they have to keep going if they are distracted. Encourage them to stay with the visualization as long as possible, and then, when they are done, let it go. Even if they don't make it all the way through, they have learned about visualization, and eventually they will be able to participate for a longer time.

Once they are done visualizing, ask them questions about how they feel. Are they more relaxed or happy? Do they feel more peaceful? Have them assess how they feel now versus how they felt before the visualization and what that means for them.

Paint it Perfect

For children who really struggle to practice visualization, they may prefer to physically visit their happy place. While it might not be possible to actually go there, painting or drawing a picture is a great opportunity for them to see their happy place in front of them; doing this can help them go there mentally. Get your child to draw or paint as many different elements of their happy place as possible. Although they may not be able to include the actual smells, sounds, and tastes, they can include the sources (such as the ocean or the forest), and think about that as they draw or paint. It is a great opportunity to bring their vision to life, especially if they are struggling to create the vision in their mind and hold onto it for a period of time.

Guide the Tribe

Another great way to help children visit their happy place is to have them guide the tribe. With this activity, they will be telling others a story about their happy place. They can either share it with you alone, or they can share it in a story circle, depending upon the environment. Instruct them to share their happy place, and if they feel stuck, give them questions to consider and answer to help other people visualize their happy place.

For example, if you are in a story circle, you may start with Johnny. Johnny may decide that his happy place that day is at his grandma's when she is baking cookies. Ask him to explain what his grandma's kitchen looks like, what his grandma looks like, and anything else he remembers. Then, you can ask him to explain what type of cookies they are, and what they smell like. You may even ask him to share what they taste like when he eats them. By doing this practice, you get the storyteller to go deeper into their happy place. You also teach kids to learn about visualization practices as they visualize someone else's happy place. Additionally, you teach them to become aware of other individuals aside from themselves and understand that everyone has their own unique life and experiences.

This activity is great for children who are not as visual as others. Those who like to talk will likely enjoy this activity. It teaches them to go deeper into their own happy place in a way that is natural and comfortable to the child. In doing so, you increase the positive association with their happy place and how they feel there. You can also encourage them to use this description as the basis for what to visualize the next time they practice visualization.

Vision Boards

Vision boards are popular among all ages for their ability to help people picture their happy place. This is an activity that serves children in many wonderful ways. It begins as an incredible craft, and then it is transformed into an excellent visualization tool.

Adults typically use vision boards to develop an idea of what they want to attract into their lives and then manifest. For children, the idea doesn't need to follow this script. Instead, you can help them develop vision boards that represent their happy place. Give them magazines full of pictures, and let them cut out the images that represent their happy place and paste them on a board. They can add words, images, and anything else that helps them visualize a place of peace and happiness. Once they're done, let the board dry. The craft in itself is a mindfulness practice as it helps kids think about what makes them feel positive in life.

Once the vision boards are dry, they provide a great opportunity for kids to learn to visualize. For children who struggle to visualize, let them use the vision board so they can see their happy place. This is a great opportunity for them to regularly revisit the things that make them happy and develop a positive association with those things. It can also teach them to generate feelings of positivity when they are struggling to feel positive. If a child is feeling overwhelmed, fearful, angry, sad, or any other stressful emotion, you can encourage them to look at their vision board and imagine that they are taking a vacation to their happy place, wherever that is. This way, they can become mindful of their present emotions and learn to create the emotions they want to create, which is a powerful skill for children to learn.

Vacationing in a happy place is not a new concept; it is something that people have done for ages. However, it is possible to modify this activity and make it functional for kids. There are many ways that you can use their happy place as an opportunity to teach them about feelings and emotions. This exercise presents a great opportunity to identify when they are feeling stressed or overwhelmed, and then to intentionally shift those emotions to something more positive. Being able to do this is a powerful skill that is highly necessary for children. The techniques in this chapter present a wonderful opportunity to help children feel more positive about life by employing a few simple strategies.

MASTERING YOUR MIND

❄

The mind is a complicated and vast place. Many areas of the mind are a mystery even to mindful people. Still, it is a place that we strive to understand and one that we desire to control on some level. Learning to do so can have a profound impact on your entire life. Many adults struggle with the process of mastering their mind, so it's no wonder that it can be considered difficult for children. But, imagine the differences of a child who learns these skills early in life, versus an adult, who starts learning them in adulthood. A child who learns techniques and begins mastering their mind at a young age will have the ability to be emotionally intelligent and resilient throughout their life. This chapter focuses on activities that help children master their minds through internal exploration.

Mini Meditation for Mini Masters

Most children are going to struggle with meditating for a long period of time, but it is still important to learn to meditate to some degree. While they may only meditate for a few minutes, any level of meditation is positive. As they learn to meditate effectively, they will eventually be able to extend the time they spend meditating until they are able to meditate easily for any time length. Meditating for about fifteen minutes at a time is optimal. Using these mini meditation practices, you will be able to teach children to meditate, and eventually they will work up to the fifteen-minute window.

Meditating with children is like teaching adults to meditate, but you need to use appropriate language. You want to teach the child to be very still and calm and to focus on their breath and body when they are meditating. As you are teaching, you can say things like, "We are going to get into our mindfulness bodies now. Are you ready?" In this way, you can teach children about their own mindfulness body. Then, you can lead them through a mini meditation practice.

Start by having children sit on chairs or on the floor with their legs crossed. If you want to really help them get into their mindfulness bodies, you can have specific carpets or pillows that they sit on when they are meditating. Sometimes, having a physical association with a specific activity can help children get in the mood for it. Then, you can ask them to quiet down. Give them a few minutes to stop chattering and being distracted. Once they are calm, you can ask them to close their eyes, and then guide them to focus on their breath. If it helps, they can put their hands on their tummies to feel them rise and fall with the breath.

Start by having the children relax in this way for a few minutes, and end the session before they become too fidgety. Once they are relaxed, you can instruct them to slowly open their eyes and bring their attention back to the room. Then, they can put their mindfulness bodies aside and resume playing when they are ready.

This activity can be performed at a routine time every day or you can practice the activity when children become rowdy. You can help bring them back to peacefulness or help remind them to pay attention to their bodies. Perhaps there is a conflict between children. You can help them meditate and then have a conversation about the conflict and teach them a lesson surrounding the conflict.

Emotion in Motion

Emotion in motion is a fun activity that can help children resolve stressful emotions. It helps them identify the emotions and the feelings they are experiencing. This opportunity allows them to understand the effect of emotions and to learn positive ways to release energy.

When a child is full of emotions, whether positive or negative, you can instruct them to stand in a certain spot. You may use a small carpet to help keep the child in a specific space. The small area carpets are ideal if you have multiple children practicing at once, as it will keep them in their own space and prevent them from invading anyone else's personal space.

Once each child is in their personal space, instruct them to start moving in the way they feel. If they are calm, they might sway from side to side. If they are angry, they might jump around or throw their hands in the air. If they have a lot of energy, they might jump on the spot. Ask them to move in whatever way feels right for the energy that they are feeling in the moment. After about a minute of moving around, ask them to stop and relax again. Then, ask the child what they felt that encouraged them to move in the way they did. Ask them to describe their feelings now that they've been moving around a bit. Children and adults alike are prone to feeling restless, and getting their bodies wiggling and moving is a great way to get rid of the emotions. You can put on music and make it like a dance party if you want. Doing this gives children an opportunity to move those emotions out and to feel calmer afterward.

Teaching children to manage their emotions in a positive way is so important, and physically working them out of their system is an important skill. It allows them to understand that there are positive and effective methods for eliminating unwanted or excessive energies from their bodies. When children learn to effectively move emotions out of their body, they may be less likely to move them out in potentially destructive or dangerous ways. This activity also helps them identify their emotions and how they make them feel.

Scan the Man

Body scans are a great way to "check in" with yourself. In virtually every mindfulness guide, there is a section that discusses the process of scanning your body for feelings and sensations. Through the process, you can identify if something feels unwell if there is a lot of energy somewhere, or if you want to send loving energy to someone. For example, if you are struggling with missing someone, you may want to send love to your heart and to that person.

Teaching children to scan their body is an incredibly important skill. It allows them to understand how they feel inside and to develop self-awareness around their emotions and feelings. When children learn to scan their bodies, they learn to identify what feels good for them and what doesn't feel good. They develop the ability to gain insight when something feels *off* or *wrong*, whether it's physically or emotionally.

To do a scanning process with children, start by getting them to meditate. Have them sit quietly and think about their breath for a few moments. Then, start asking them questions about their bodies starting at the top of the head. Ask them to silently answer the questions in their mind as they focus on the questions you are asking. Tell them that they will get the chance to share their answers later. Ask how each body part feels from the top of their head down to the bottom of their feet. Go slowly enough to give them time to pay attention to that area on their body but quickly enough to keep them from getting distracted. Most children will answer the question in a few seconds, so you can keep going at a fairly consistent pace.

Once the scan is done, ask the children to focus on the breath for a few more seconds before they open their eyes. Then, ask them to tell you what they noticed. If there are many children, start with one and go around the circle. Give them the opportunity to tell you how they felt, if they noticed something felt really good or not so good, and anything else they might have noticed. Once they are done telling you, ask deeper questions to teach them how to look further into those emotions or feelings. Ask them why they think they have that feeling. If the feelings are discomfort or other unwanted feelings, ask them if they can identify one or two ways that they could prevent those feelings or emotions in the future. Also, ask them if they think there is any way that they could heal those emotions or feelings in a positive way now that they have identified them. This process helps them understand the purpose of the body scan and how they can use this process to identify their emotions and practice problem-solving skills, when necessary. If the child feels totally awesome everywhere, encourage them to celebrate that feeling!

Passing Clouds

Thoughts, emotions, feelings and more flow through the mind on a regular basis. When children are in the process of learning about these things, it can be beneficial to play passing clouds. Passing clouds teaches children not to dwell on thoughts, feelings or emotions that are not beneficial. When they play passing clouds, they learn to let thoughts pass by like a cloud, making it possible to recognize the thought, recognize the feelings it brings up, and then recognize them going away. While this won't necessarily heal things that may be deeply affecting them; it will allow them to move on from the things that are not serving them.

At first, children may only be able to attach their thoughts to the clouds. There may be no awareness of the emotions or feelings attached to those thoughts. Over time, however, they will learn how to attach the emotions and feelings to the clouds and let them pass by.

To play passing clouds, start by having children sit down and relax.

Once they are calm, have them take a few breaths. If they are distracted or fidgety, have them count five breaths or count to five for them to keep them focused. Then, you can instruct them to imagine a clear, blue sky with big fluffy clouds passing by. Once they are picturing the sky, have them imagine that each thought is one of the clouds. They can picture the thought inside of the cloud, somewhat like a thought bubble in a graphic novel. Then, once the picture of the thought is in the cloud, they can imagine it sliding away as a new cloud comes in. Each time a thought comes up, they can put it into one of the clouds and let it go.

Keep doing this with a few clouds and then end the session. Each time you do this practice, add a few more clouds until they're doing between 10-15 clouds or whatever is comfortable for them. Then, end the session. The point is to teach kids to learn to let things go. When things upset or frustrate them, teach them that it's okay to let thoughts or clouds slide by and focus on things that are more positive. The intention is *not* to teach them to ignore problems or things that may be troubling them, so make sure that they are clear on what the differences are.

Exploring their inner selves and developing a sense of self-awareness is important for children. It teaches them that they are important and that their feelings, emotions, and thoughts are important. They also learn how to absorb the information from these thoughts, feelings, and emotions and then let them go. The various processes teach them the importance of the self and how they can lead a more positive and healthy life when they are able to examine their own body and problem-solve, when necessary, in a healthy way.

TEACHING TRICKS

❄

Teaching children mindfulness practices can be difficult if you are not sure where to start. The practices in this book intend to teach children to relax and develop a mindfulness practice of their own. With these tricks, the entire process can be easy, and you can explain it to your child or children. The tricks or tips eliminate the frustration and confusion when trying to communicate these practices and the importance of teaching children. The tips make the process more enjoyable.

Tip #1: Understand Mindfulness Yourself

Before you try to teach mindfulness to children, make sure you understand it yourself. Understanding mindfulness, as well as developing your own practice, will help immensely when it comes to teaching it to children. The knowledge will allow you to stay calm and focused throughout the practice, and will also help you make it easy for children. You certainly don't need to be a master at mindfulness, but you should spend a little time practicing it before you teach children.

Tip #2: Keep Everything Simple

If you want children to understand what you are teaching them, keep everything simple. The practices should not be elaborate or advanced. For adults, several minutes' worth of meditation practices may be acceptable, but for children, several minutes may be too much. Keep the activities short and easy to understand. Instead of several minutes of meditation, practice meditating for a minute or two and then stop. When they get used to that, move it up to about five minutes. For children who want to meditate longer, of course, they can. For others who feel comfortable with this level, it is completely fine to leave it there.

Tip #3: Lower Your Expectations

It is important that you go into mindfulness practices and conduct them with the right expectations and intentions. The purpose of these practices is not to teach children in a few sessions how to perfectly meditate for 15 minutes. In reality, the children may not ever master the specific practices you are teaching them. However, they will learn something and they will benefit. As they grow older and develop a greater understanding for what you are teaching them, they will go on to master even more. The point is not to have mini mindfulness masters walking around by seven, eight, nine or even ten years of age. The expectation should be that you are helping them learn a little about mindfulness and with each session their learning will increase. The total amount of learned information will vary between children, but the purpose remains the same. Anything they learn will be valuable.

Tip #4: Focus On the Process, Not the Outcome

Elaborating on the previous tip, you should take the time to focus on the process of the mindfulness practices and not the outcome. While the goal should be maintained, the emphasis should be on the practice. Take the time necessary to explain each practice to the best of your ability. Help children do it to the best of their ability, too. Let them learn as much as they can. If it's too much, slow down. If it's not enough, ramp it up. Pay attention to the child and what they need. Although the outcome is important, taking the emphasis off of the outcome can make the process less stressful and can help emphasize the lessons and not the answers.

Tip #5: Don't Force Anything

Make sure you do everything at the child's pace. If three minutes is too much, slow down. If three minutes is not enough, practice more. For children who do not like stillness practices, use practices that include motion. If a child is artistic, use something like a vision board or a sensory bag to help maintain their focus through the practice. Always follow the child's lead. The process should be enjoyable. You want the child or children to have a positive association with mindfulness practices so that when they are ready, they are eager to learn more.

Tip #6: Practice Regularly

Practice on a regular basis is important for anyone who is learning mindfulness strategies. Whether you practice once every day or once every week, practicing frequently will help children learn. As they want to, they will ask for more. Eventually, you will probably notice that they start practicing the strategies you teach them on their own time. The point is to help them develop their own mindfulness practice at a young age so that they can improve on that in time. Mindfulness will help them learn important problem-solving and social skills from understanding, managing, and processing their emotions. The more they practice, the more they will learn.

Tip #7: Use Their Language

You cannot talk to children in adult language and expect them to understand what you are saying. You will need to take your time and teach them what mindfulness using their language. You might explain to them that "mindfulness is a tool we use to understand our emotions" instead of "mindfulness is a practice to develop emotional intelligence." Adjust your language to suit the age of the child so they can understand and stay engaged. If you lose them before you even start, you will struggle to teach them anything.

Tip #8: Keep It Fun

It is very important to keep the process fun for children. For adults, the idea of 15 minutes of pure quietness can seem like a treat. For children, it may seem torturous. Ensure that your techniques and language make the process fun for them. This way, you can keep their attention and make the practice a positive experience. The more fun they have, the more they will want to practice mindfulness.

Teaching children how to be mindful has a powerful effect on their lives. Learning how to do so requires practice and effort, but once you understand how to successfully teach mindfulness to children you will likely see a profound effect in a relatively short time. The longer you practice with them, the more significant the effect will be. Remember to keep it fun, focus on the experience, and make it enjoyable for them, and you will be fine!

CONCLUSION

❄

Mindfulness is a beneficial practice for anyone. Teaching it to children puts them ahead in life, as it teaches them self-awareness, emotional intelligence, and social skills. Children who learn about mindfulness are more likely to have a successful social life, since they can identify and manage their emotions. They are less likely to be affected by bullies. They generally have a healthier overall mental wellness state, which can be powerful for children who are going through the difficult stages of hormonal changes and development.

Teaching mindfulness to children can be fun for the teacher and the child. There are many ways to turn mindfulness into enjoyable games that effectively teach these skills. When you use mindfulness practices that appeal to children, you increase their involvement and enjoyment from the practice, as well as the skills they gain from it. The main thing is to understand that when teaching children, you will need to slow down and practice mindfulness in a way that appeals to them.

I hope this book will help you teach mindfulness to children. When you are in the process, remember to take your time and use language that appeals to children. If one way isn't working, try another. Take it slowly and stay focused on the experience more than the goal. Children tend to understand these practices effortlessly once it becomes a regular part of their routine.

The next step is to discover what practices appeal to them at their present stage. Once you do, you can introduce the concept of mindfulness in a way that they will understand, and then start incorporating it into their daily schedule. Take your time and make it fun, and they will quickly start looking forward to the mindfulness practice. Remember not to force anything, and make the pace appropriate for children. This will make it the most beneficial, as it will attach a positive association to the mindfulness experience. They will likely start practicing it on their own if they find that the practices benefit them.

Lastly, if you enjoyed this book, would you please leave a review for Amazon Kindle users? I would appreciate your honest feedback.

Thank you, and best of luck!

FREE BONUS

*** Limited-Time FREE Kindle Book For You ***

>>> Get it NOW FREE >>>

BookHip.com/RAZGNH

21 FUN indoor games
for kids

Camelia Gherib

How many times have you heard the phrase, "I'm so bored" on a rainy day or even worse on a sunny day? Are you ever tempted to plop your children in front of the TV or a video game system?

Perhaps you feel you have tried it all. Maybe your kids have never liked games. Are you out of fun ideas to try? Whatever your situation you are sure to find some amazing games in this book!

Press Here and Get Your FREE Copy NOW!

BookHip.com/RAZGNH

ABOUT THE AUTHOR

Camelia Gherib is the author/illustrator of over a dozen traditionally published books for children.

Camelia combines humour and ethical messages in a pedagogical way that appeal to the hearts of children and entertain parents.

For more information:

www.thehappyfamily.co

camelia@thehappyfamily.co

Mindfulness for Children: 21 Fun Exercises for Children to Increase Attention Span and Improve Social Skills and Mental Health

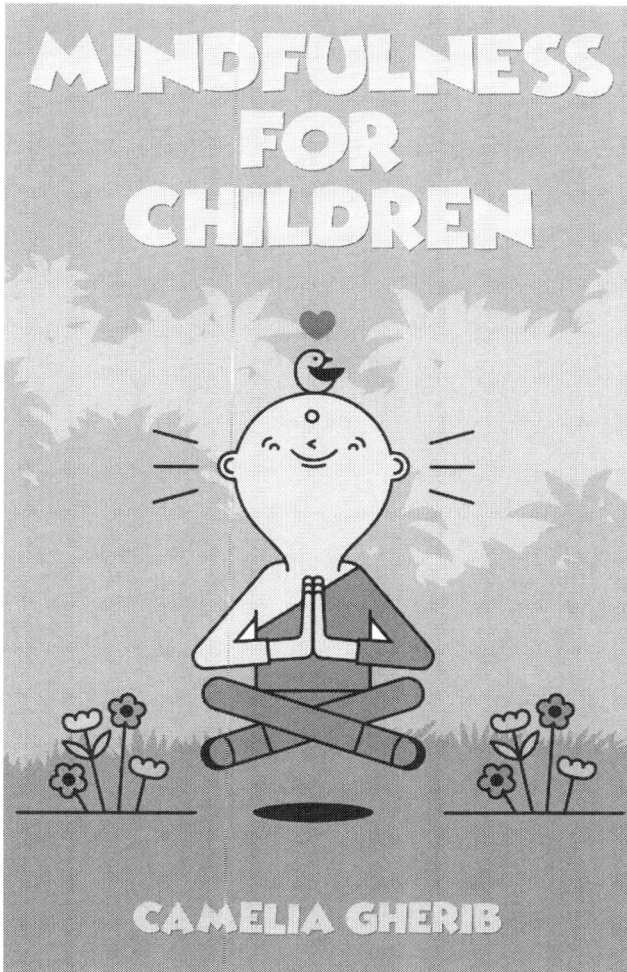

Meditation: 21-Day Simple Meditation Techniques To Inner Peace, Love & Joy

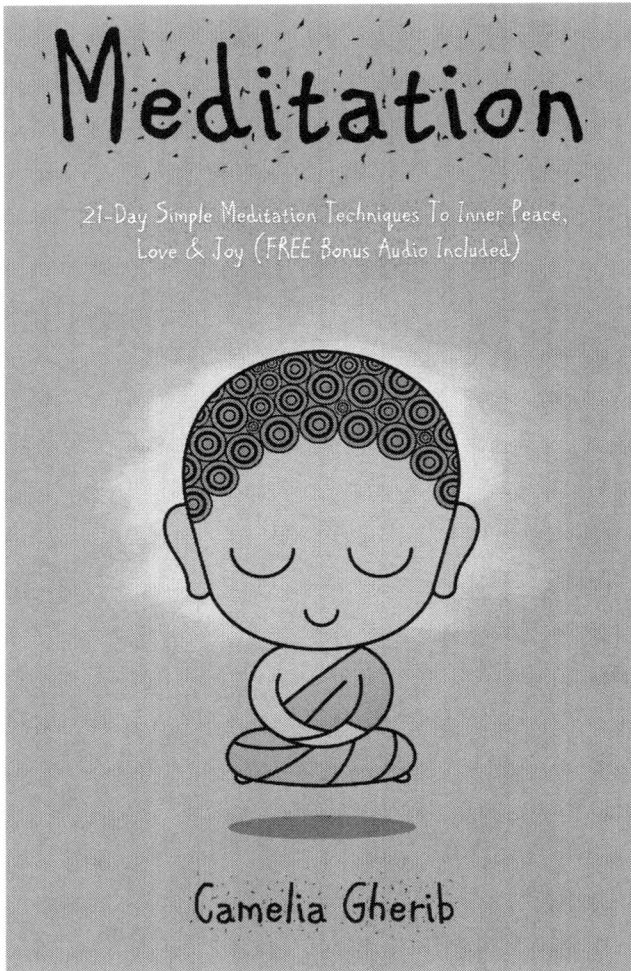

Indoor Games: 21 Fun Indoor Games for Kids

21 FUN
indoor games
for kids

Camelia Gherib

How Jerry Giraffe Got His Spots

CAMELIA GHERIB

HOW JERRY GIRAFFE GOT HIS SPOTS

FURTHER READING

Here is a list of other book titles I have read and found immensely interesting:

Sitting Still Like a Frog: Mindfulness Exercises for Kids- By Eline Snel

A Handful of Quiet: Happiness in Four Pebbles- By Thich Nhat Hanh

Good Night Yoga: A Pose-by-Pose Bedtime Story- By Mariam Gates

Peaceful Piggy Meditation- By Kerry Lee Maclean

I Am Yoga - By Susan Verde

Printed in Great Britain
by Amazon